AF263972

VICTORY'S JUDGE

VICTORY'S JUDGE

Ian Bloom

Natural

IAN BLOOM

Ian Bloom is an art dealer and founder of Natural Gallery.

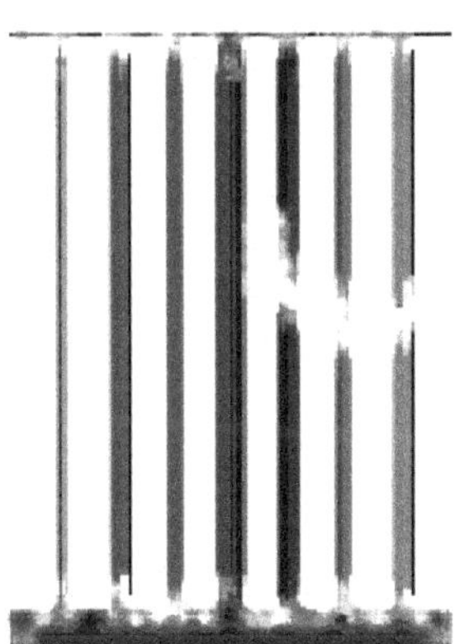

VICTORY'S JUDGE

"Freeway"

Nothing came against.
Closers in the morning,
She said, she'd like
        a sunrise.
And that was the
        day before
        yesterday.

"Merge Left"

Knobs, doors, shadows,
the boxes.

Rain breaking concrete
Scoring,
Missing she and
        all her variations.

"Cars"

You ravish the vanishing point.

Natural and purposeful
and calm.

You're so special.
You're not going to see the sides and you'll just
set in motion and
all that perpetual strife will
suffocate your sorrows.

Isolation is an open
space devoid of barriers
and darkness.

Feel the wood you step on.

It's softer than stone.

"Replace muse"

Replace muse, the word,
it's too general.
Conjure an image,
not a type,
a person, a
soul,
one innocuous
possessive of
personal bravado, and
charm disguised as innocence.
Mean streaks masked in decorous ubiquity.
Universal beauty,
Internal strife,
Naked via gazes,
proxied by curves and motions,
mostly the moments before
Truth, when the smile only comes
after the seduction.
For she encapsulates with
no limits to

the description.

"Pretending you're not aroused"

The book of any love is a vat of cooling water
steaming with waste products.
It's necessary to exorcise the vitriol for appearances'
sake.
So what happens to be pure, or sublime, if you dare dub it,
can be smile worthy.
Because you declare you love her, and you call her, babe,
and, maybe you'll have you for me.
All in nothing,
Her smiles, her feet bare, and exposed the way the light
strikes
her muscles in motion. Fuck the fucking feet.

The way her skin feels like ocean
you're already one with ethereal beyond body.
That's what you wish it came down to,
because we're all clowns dying accelerated to
encouragement,
and we gravitate to possibility.
No matter, she has magic magnetism and any one who drinks
the cool syrup has already done
a more commendable job in expression
than I can expect.

"In the Way"

An ode to what strikes may long lover's eyes
lock in to wander.

'Tis not the care to caress
that crashes waves of lucidity
and mystery,
but the spaces between the legs,
governed by the structures of
ordinance and custom.

For, if her leg points wayward
after such steady target,
is it not due to the resonance
of mature words or the
potent potential catharsis.

Was the lips on the cheeks, half meant
to be ambiguous yet so
pure and true. For truth may be fickle
but the longing to express it is
lovely nonetheless.

"Asinine Reminders I"

Halt.
Oil infused chariots.
Burn, pillage, worship the light.

Carry on West wayward wearing to the white noise.
Wisdom of the harlots.

Ye shall be guided in strips folding nowhere constant and
tangible
like a cloud crashing mist over a salt deficient sanctuary.
Rub each other's bellies.
Drink up.
Harrow to hearken seismic trembling solely situated
beyond dilations pumping streams into pools
for pleasure.
For the way of the Gun is absolute and nothing can deny
absolute.

"Asinine Reminders II"

Diffuse the specter. Raunchy undertones distinguish
tortoise steps.
Letting it ride and lithe tiny tunes.
Tourniquets are a consumer staple.
Metal armor screams archaic atrocity.
Terrorize your body and
ye shall contaminate through storms permeating the dying
dermis.

Carnage caves reserve this right, and to not only find one,
yet, choose to enter, beware the call of the civilized. If
ye dare,
remember that it is ye for whom the wolves cry
and the cubs clamor,
Feed me,
Feed me,
Feed me.

"Idiots"

He spoke in mud
and he looked at walls.
Intonating garbage painted glittery
showcasing who was in charge.

Obvious to no one except her delusions,
she listened to imitate.
And she got off on her chaste coy ploy,
to prey on a mind
sedate in sin.

Remote webs broke
and if he was not such a mudslinger, silence
could slingshot an animal forward
over that vacuous shenanigan
of sabotage between.

Space had a sham.
Until he destructed her.
Pleasure's nihilist.

"Brandishing the Sword"

She said she loved me
and that her wish was
I'd never leave.

The whiskey talked
Miss Wonderful up into
caveats of resistance, for
each declaration intonated
to ice the shackles of
the puritan's heart.

For, was he to breach
and negate the valves built and
embedded into the beauty's
dynamism.

They loved that
they could not, yet
it made it all the more
desirable and devious,
a garden forked into levels
with mirrored shades of glass
and reflecting pools of
devout voids.

The way it was
was isolate,
sterile,
sad.

And she was the hope for
never more
could be
no faith in any better
before such a quandary.

If only he was engaged
to pleasure,
screwed away any portrayal
of romance.

But she knew he was dangerous in role
and capable in dreams.

She could not take his away
and it was a match at stalemate.

The pangs of honor
harbored resentment, recoil
to misery, blood, smoke,
and apathetic content.

For nonexistence only reinforced
the triviality in desire.

To desire her
was to suffer,
and each admission
only let her awareness fester
into caution, wary minstrels
poking at her nature.

Dying, she would not be,
a shame the times had damned.

The doorway to
destruction was the only option.

He always had the keys
and she'd be gone through
the dearth of reality.

Such a shame,
he wished she'd change.
And it'd be up,
if he wasn't so scared to take,
snatch.

It'd only be heaven and he'd wade
through hell to gorge a treasure
to build her castle of never.

Never, never, never,
that was a saving absolute, alone
as a seed without the base to grow
and live.

Lost against the bricks built and
swallowed into the burial that
description dedicated.

He had class, cool, virility.

So, break her mold,
reduced to romance,
actual for real.

Hope was an everlasting cigarette scarring
his heart immobile.

If he decided, what more to think.
Pathetic.
Masochist.

Drop your trousers.
Touch her hips.

Some day when it's night
and it's sober
and she decides
it's you.

If it's a dream,
then it's always going to be dead.

Change that
and banish the forces.
Is it so grim that he must take and take
what he desires, the endless cycle of
commandment seizure.

Trading turmoil instead of tender orgasm.
Play the dream to win, make it a comedy
and then, she's yours.

Act the role.
Ascend.
Be a man, and time orders the inevitable.

She's always,
she's going,
wait it out.
It's a road.
The destination
comforts the point,
as you vanish.

"Rigging Roulette"

Come cobble my cornstick,
felonious.

Eat my spit and
drink my air.

In spite of your
Spartan semantical
pigshit.

I preferred you
as a prude.

Now, it's quickly
shifting color until it'll all be
united in a tepid mess.

Looking at pedantic
still lifes
absent of skill
and clarity,
homesteading classic civility.

Cobweb your ass,
I may, if you
have the decency to open the door
naked, so I don't have to shave
beforehand.

Ruination is target practice.

Skull fuck.

Fucking freeze.

Gnaw.
Over with it.

I'm already died
in the unity of the mixed colors.

Hondo.

I enjoy the name. I
hate it when you say it.

If you were not such a perfect
colt, I'd have vanished before
you could carry me to waters
that have me choking coarse
smut song shameless in vitros.

You should get a job,
so I can die next to you
and cool your flame.

I already drew you
and painted you
and sculpted you
and burnt it all
to a black crisp,
for no good good enough.

The gravestone will say
I embraced the mystery
and
once I found it,
I let you chop off
my limbs.

Nike took nothing, all
by accident.

I love you.

Do the twist.

"Full Stomach"

Stony bores shirking,
saying the weather
        is nice today,
oblivious to their
        cries for help.
Help, Help. I need
        a jolt. I'm so
        lonely. Oh, just look
        at me and my nude eyes
        and my mirth masking
        fear.

Let's be friends.
See, my friends, hear
the hordes hurting
        and circling the
        globe in gargantuan
        toil.

I know better, am
        no better.
Call a gamble a dissociation
        with reality.
Call a man a name
        recognition of
        yes or no.

Fuck off, the whole lot.

"Bad Bad Bad, Bad Bad"

Bad guy.
In love with
this girl and she
surely felt my
force at work.
And then we have
fights and we stop.

Bad guy.
Learn her
dependent
situation
dealer.

Especially bad guy.
Friends.
Screw around.
Take off.
Liberation.

No wreckage.
Wisdom weak.
Certain style.
Beseech the
degenerate.
Sad truth.
No mind,
nothing happened,
or it didn't.
Wide.

Natural